Magic Words

Words With Special Meanings

by

Erdine Savage Njie

AuthorHouse™
1663 Liberty Drive
Bloomington, IN 47403
www.authorhouse.com
Phone: 833-262-8899

Because of the dynamic nature of the Internet, any web addresses or links contained in
this book may have changed since publication and may no longer be valid. The views
expressed in this work are solely those of the author and do not necessarily reflect the views
of the publisher, and the publisher hereby disclaims any responsibility for them.

This book is printed on acid-free paper.

ISBN: 978-1-4259-0575-0 (sc)
ISBN: 978-1-4678-5119-0 (e)

Print information available on the last page.

Published by AuthorHouse 04/22/2022

authorHOUSE®

This book is dedicated to my vanilla angel, Keith.
To my sister Erma Smith who wrote the book on love.
To my son Benjamin Njie who allowed my inner child to play.
Last, but not least, Dr. Barbara Lewis King, my minister who
taught me that believing is seeing!

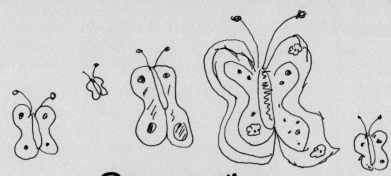

Butterflies

When a butterfly is in its cocoon does it know or care
what colors its wings will be?

Color doesn't matter when you can fly!
It's what's inside that count.

Jack and Jill

Jack and Jill went up the hill to get a pail of water. Jack fell
down and broke his crown and Jill took out her cell phone
and called 911

911 is an important number to know!

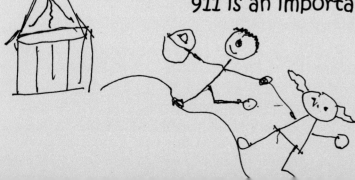

A Bird

A bird flew through the window one day. He couldn't find a way out. We opened all the windows and doors. Finally, after a very long time, he found an open window and soared through. I feel like that sometimes when I do math at school.
If I keep trying to find the answer, suddenly I get it and like the bird, I sprout wings and fly!

It's important to be PERSISTENT.

4 Eyes

Some kids call me four eyes because I wear glasses. That means I have 2 more eyes than they do, but just like Superman I wear my glasses to protect my super vision.

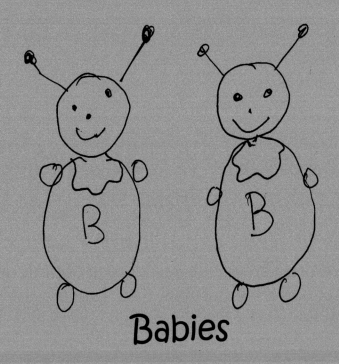

Babies

My baby brother is brand new. He cries a lot and looks funny. Is he a real person or just pretending? Could he be an alien?

Angels

Are there really angels? I've never seen one, Maybe, BELIEVING is seeing!

A. D. H. D.

Attention **D**eficit **H**yperactivity **D**isorder

Attention Deficit Hyperactivity Disorder

My doctor said I have ADHD, that's the reason I can't stop moving, but
I really think it means
Always   Doing   Happy   Deeds
,
I just do them faster than others.

Peace

People Everywhere Acting Calm Everyday
PEACE

Doll House

I have a very pretty dollhouse. But the windows are too small, I can't see inside. My mother said, I should use my imagination to see inside. She was right I can see better. I guess I should use my imagination to eat my brussels sprouts too (yuck) Maybe I should try looking through the door.

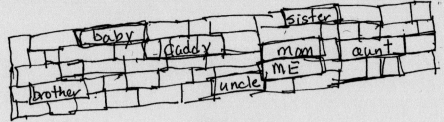

Bricks

The other day I saw a man building a house with red bricks. I watched him as he carefully placed the bricks together using this gray stuff called cement. He said the cement helps the bricks stay together. My mom and dad are the cement that holds my family together.
How about you?

ICE CREAM

Who ate all the vanilla ice cream?
I can't hear you! I got too much vanilla in my ears!

Inner Child

Who drank all the orange juice? I don't know. Maybe it was my inner child.

orange juice

Thanksgiving

It is a tradition in my family to celebrate Thanksgiving by giving a food basket to the homeless. We take the basket down to the shelter. Sometimes we help serve but I wonder what happens to the homeless people between January and November?
I know, they go into hibernation.

Food for Thought

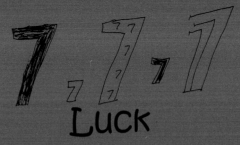

Playground

The other day I fell on the playground. I hurt my knee. The kids laughing at me hurt more

Sticks and stones might break your bones but words hurt too.

Luck

Someone said number 7 is a lucky number. Does that mean all the other numbers are unlucky? What is luck anyway? I think luck is when we haven't found a way to explain how God did it.

Toes

I saw a man today with one of his toes missing. I asked him what happened. He said, "Toes are like families. Even if one is missing the rest can still stay together and support you.

I miss my grandma.

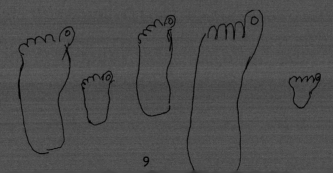

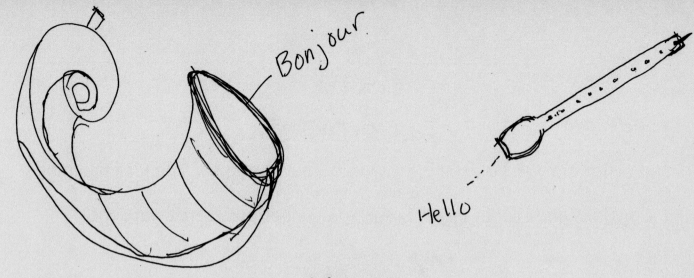

Bonjour.

Hello

Horns

Does a French horn speak French? Are there English horns? If so, are they Bi-lingual?

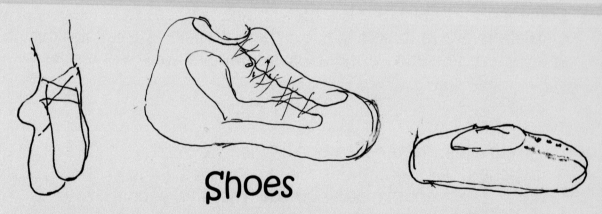

Shoes

I got shoes you got shoes. All God's children got shoes. Today I am thankful for my shoes. Shoes that help me run fast and jump high.

How beautiful are thy feet with shoes
Song of Solomon 7:1

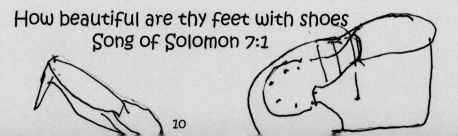

Uniforms

Next year my school has decided we will all wear uniforms. I don't know why we must all look alike. Since I was in Kindergarten my teacher told me to think for myself, and be independent. Now, is dressing alike suppose to make us all the same?

Don't be fooled by appearances.

Nerd

The other day somebody called me a nerd. What is a NERD? I asked some of my friends but they couldn't tell me. Maybe because they are nerds too. So, I decided that if I am a NERD, then it must mean
NEVER
ENGAGING (in) RIDICULES DRAMA
Always turn a negative into a positive.

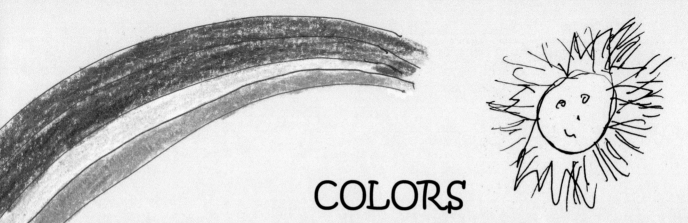

COLORS

My favorite color is orange. You mix red and yellow to get orange. If you look at the colors in nature you will see all types of colors mixing to make more colors. I've seen yellow flowers with purple stamens and fish with blue stripes and green fins. All these colors seen to blend and get along well. So why is it when we have PTA night at school and all the different colored parents come, they don't mix or talk to each other?

I can't hear what you're saying because your actions are speaking louder.

POPCORN

Have you ever noticed when you cook just a little bit of popcorn, you get a big bowl of popcorn. How does that happen?

Fishes and Loaves

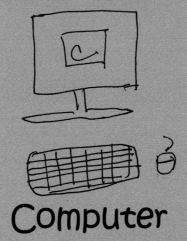

Computer

I like computers. You can do a lot of things with them like playing games doing, homework, and e-mail. but my brother is at the computer all the time. He thinks it's REAL. I tried to explain the word Artificial Intelligence.

Where's the dictionary?

The Gingerbread Man

What really happened to the Gingerbread Man? I know he ran away from a bunch on folks so how did the wolf eat him? He decided to ride across the river on the wolf's back rather then walk around.
Never take a ride from a stranger especially if it's a wolf.

FLOWERS

In the morning the flowers in our garden slowly start opening as if waiting for their first bottle. By noon they are in full bloom and start sunbathing. Then as the sun slowly starts to set their petal begin to close as if putting on their pajamas and saying good night. They do all of this without an alarm clock.

This story is brought to you courtesy, of Mother Nature!

A Funny and Long Words

Supercalafragalisticespialidosious
Is this a real word?

Ask Mary Poppins?

Test Tube Baby

What is a Test Tube Baby?
A baby who needs to take a test before being born.

Grades

Sometimes when I get bad grades I pretend the F is for FANTASTIC and the A is for Acne. Either way my mom doesn't buy it. A one legged A is still a F.

Humpty Dumpty

At school they call me Humpty Dumpty, because I'm fat. He might have
been fat like me but I bet he had strong muscles
to climb that wall.

MUSCLES

DREAM CATCHER

If a dream catcher catches your dreams
does it catch your nightmares too?
I hope so?

Litterbug

Why do they call people who throw paper and trash on the ground litterbugs? I've never seen a real bug litter. It's not like a bug can go into a store, buy a candy bar then throw the wrapper on the ground. Maybe they should call them litterpeople.

Keep America Beautiful don't litter.

Nicknames

I hate my nickname.
I don't want to be called Pee Pee Girl anymore. Why can't they change the P to pretty or popular or just use my real name PRICILLA?
I could be pretty, popular, PRICILLA!

OSTRICHES

An ostrich is a bird that can't fly. Why then do they call it a bird? Have you ever heard of a real bird that couldn't fly? Maybe the O in Ostrich should stand for ONLY. THE ONLY BIRD THAT CAN'T FLY!

POINTLESS

If something is pointless, why does it have a point at all?

Do you get the point?

Oxymoron

An Oxymoron is a figure of speech in which two words of opposite meanings are used together.
The Oxymoron I would like to use with my teacher is a warring pacifist. When teaching and giving out grades, she is warring but when it comes to parent conferences, she's very much a pacifist.

Need the dictionary Again?

Dog (Sam)

My dog Sam had to be put to sleep today. Why do they say put to sleep, when he's never going to wake up? Why don't they just say he's gone to doggy heaven to be with God?

DIAMONDS

Diamonds are a Girl's best friend!
My father bought me a pair of diamond earrings for my sixteenth birthday. They were beautiful, but I lost them. I cried and cried. My eyes were so red and swollen, until I could barely see my father when he arrived from work. I was so afraid he would be upset and would never speak to me again. Or, he would stop being my dad.
None of that happened. He said, "You are more important than those diamonds".
So, guess who my best friend is now?
My DAD
My Father
Mr. Smith
My mother's husband
The Chef

Trees

I was riding in the country with my family and I saw these trees all together like in a group or bunch. When the wind blew, they all swayed together as if holding each other up. Not once did I see one tree swaying or growing alone. I wonder if we should be more like those trees. When the wind of hard times blows we should all sway together.

Could that be the reason trees live so long?

No Child Left Behind

What does No Child Left Behind mean? I heard some of the teachers talking about it at school. I think it means when we have a field trip all the students in my class must go, even the ones who don't have enough points.

BULLY

The word BULLY stands for:

Brutes   Using   Life   Like   a Yoyo
You know what happens to a yoyo when the string breaks.

FEAR

Facing Every Appearance Ready!

Magic Words

Hocus Pocus are magic words. So are Please and Thank You.

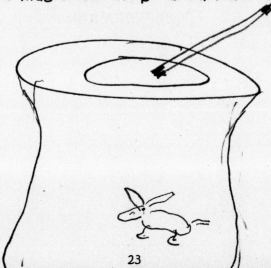

Mad Cow Disease

Who made the cows mad? Since ice cream comes from cow's milk does that mean there's no more ice cream?
Where is the cow counselor? Do they need a class in Anger Management?

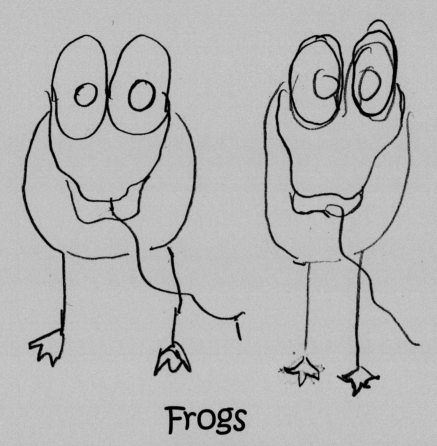

Frogs

You would think with those long tongues the could talk
Ribbit, Ribbit

About the Author

Erdine Savage Njie is a speech and language pathologist/ special education consultant in a private practice in Atlanta, Georgia. She is a native of California via Memphis, Tennessee where she was born. Presently, she resides in Atlanta with her son Benjamin.

Erdine has three advanced degrees and numerous certifications. She has received numerous awards, was featured in an article in Essence Magazine, holds two United States Copyrights for graphic drawings and soft sculptures, and was selected Outstanding Young Woman of American in 1982. She is currently pursuing another degree and desires to take her book and creative teaching skills on the road.

Printed in the United States
by Baker & Taylor Publisher Services